Can You Hear a Rainbow?

*The Story of a
Deaf Boy Named Chris*

The Rehabilitation Institute of Chicago Learning Book Series

FROM THE WESLEY M. AND SUZANNE S. DIXON EDUCATION AND TRAINING CENTER

The Making of My Special Hand: Madison's Story
Rolling Along: The Story of Taylor and His Wheelchair
Can You Hear a Rainbow?: The Story of a Deaf Boy Named Chris

Dedicated to Dr. Henry Betts, Dr. Don Olson, and Dr. Yeongchi Wu at the Rehabilitation Institute of Chicago
who inspired me with their dedication and love for educating people about disabilities.

Special Thanks

To Dr. Patricia Scherer, Ph.D., President of the International Center on Deafness and the Arts, Northbrook, Illinois, for introducing me to many remarkable children.
To Bobbi, Steve, Robyn, and Christopher Schroeder along with Tracey, Michael, and Samantha Williams for their contribution to the creation of this book.
To the young participants in the book, my beautiful children Dominic, Grant, and Gianna, and their cousins Sean, Amanda, and Sofia.
To Dr. Mary Margaret Sharp-Pucci, Ph.D., who inspired me with the title of this book.
To my husband, Bobby, for giving me the most precious gift on earth, our children. I cherish your continuous support, guidance, and everlasting love.

—*J. R. H.*

Dedicated to my parents, Dennis and Beryl Simmonds, my brother Ian, and my dear husband Matthew Carmack.

—*N. S.*

Ω

Published by
PEACHTREE PUBLISHERS, LTD.
1700 Chattahoochee Avenue
Atlanta, GA 30318-2112

www.peachtree-online.com

Book design by Nicola Simmonds and Matthew Carmack
Original photography by Jamee Riggio Heelan

Printed in Singapore

10 9 8 7 6 5 4 3 2 1
First Edition

Library of Congress Cataloging-in-Publication Data
Heelan, Jamee Riggio.
   Can you hear a rainbow? : the story of a deaf boy named Chris / Jamee Riggio Heelan ; illustrations by Nicola Simmonds.-- 1st ed.
      p. cm. -- (A Rehabilitation Institute of Chicago learning book)
   Summary: A deaf child tells how he uses sign language, hearing aids, and his other senses to communicate, how his friends help him, and how he goes to public school with an interpreter.
      ISBN 1-56145-268-8
   1. Deaf children--Juvenile literature. 2. Deaf children--Means of communication--Juvenile literature. 3. Deafness--Juvenile literature.
   [1. Deaf. 2. Physically handicapped. 3. Sign language.] I. Simmonds, Nicola, ill. II. Title. III. Series.
      HV2392 .H44 2002
      362.4'2'092--dc21
                                                            2001006165
                                                                   Rev.

A Rehabilitation Institute of Chicago Learning Book

Can You Hear a Rainbow?

*The Story of a
Deaf Boy Named Chris*

**Jamee Riggio Heelan, OTR/L
Rehabilitation Institute of Chicago**

Illustrations by Nicola Simmonds

PEACHTREE
ATLANTA

Hi, my name is Chris. When I was a baby, my parents

sensed that I was different from my brothers and my sister.

They noticed that I didn't wake up when our dog barked

and I didn't jump when the door slammed.

My parents took me to the

doctor, and he tested my

ears. He said because my

ears couldn't hear sounds

that most people can hear,

I was deaf.

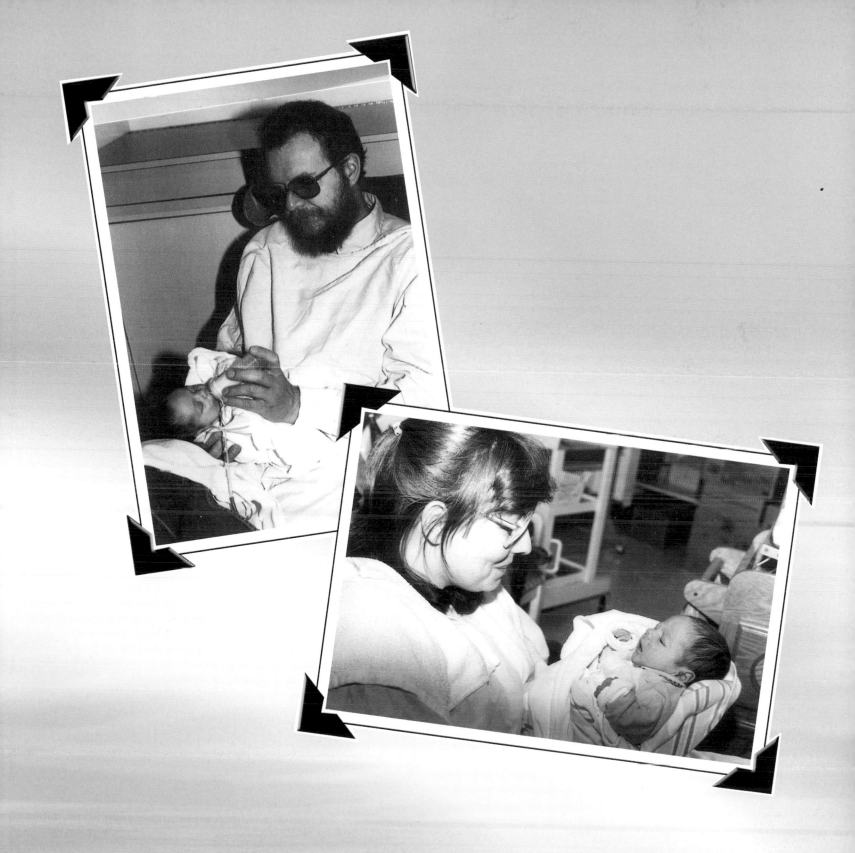

I can't hear simple sounds like the pitter-patter of rain hitting my bedroom window, the song on my sister's music box, or the telephone ringing. I can't even hear my parents' voices.

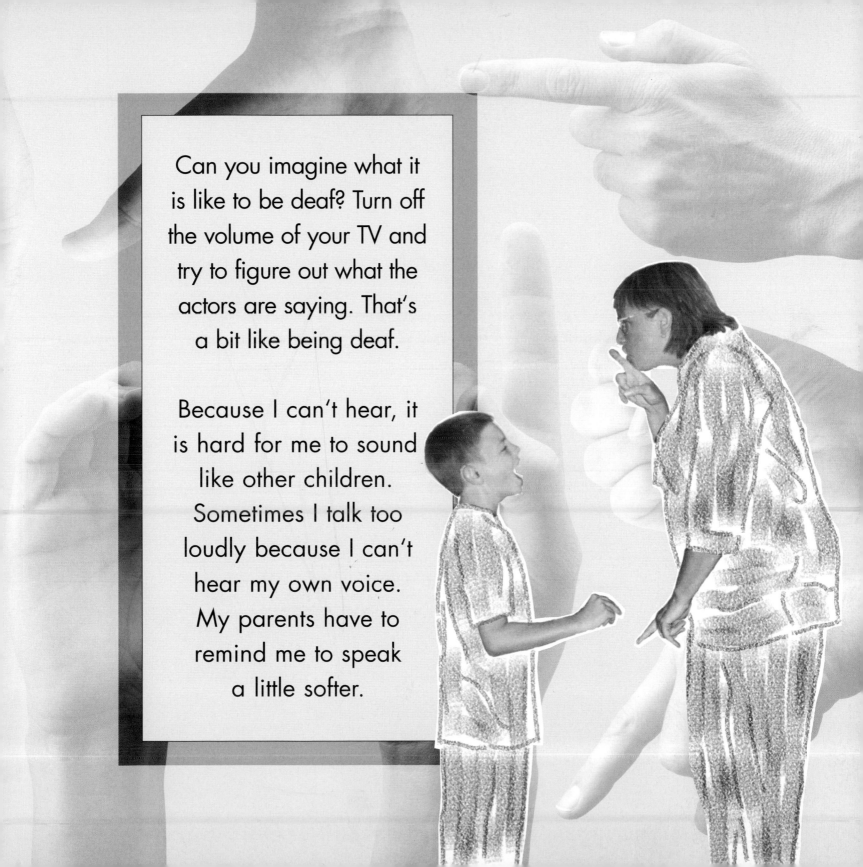

Can you imagine what it is like to be deaf? Turn off the volume of your TV and try to figure out what the actors are saying. That's a bit like being deaf.

Because I can't hear, it is hard for me to sound like other children. Sometimes I talk too loudly because I can't hear my own voice. My parents have to remind me to speak a little softer.

When I was a year old, my doctor referred me to an audiologist. She fitted me with hearing aids. The tiny microphones inside them pick up sounds and make them seem louder to me. The hearing aids don't take away my deafness or help me talk. But they do help me hear vibrations of loud noises and high-pitched sounds like the siren of a fire engine passing by.

Even with my hearing aids, I still can't hear very many sounds, so I use other ways to communicate with my family and friends. When I was little, my parents learned a way of talking called "sign language" and then taught it to my brothers, my sister, and me.

With our fingers and hands, we can form words and sentences. This special language lets me talk to other people who know how to sign.

Dogs can understand sign language, too. I taught my dog, Summer, the signs for sit and stay.

With the help of hearing aids and sign language, I understood a lot. But I still couldn't talk with people who didn't know how to sign. I saw a speech therapist once a week to learn how to "lip read." She taught me to watch the way her lips moved so I could understand the words she was speaking. Now I can "listen" to my friends with my eyes.

I don't need to hear to know what's going on around me. I know when dinner is ready by the smells coming from our kitchen. I'm usually the first one at the table because my nose gives me a head start!

And when I spot my brother's hockey equipment by the door, I know he has a game that day.

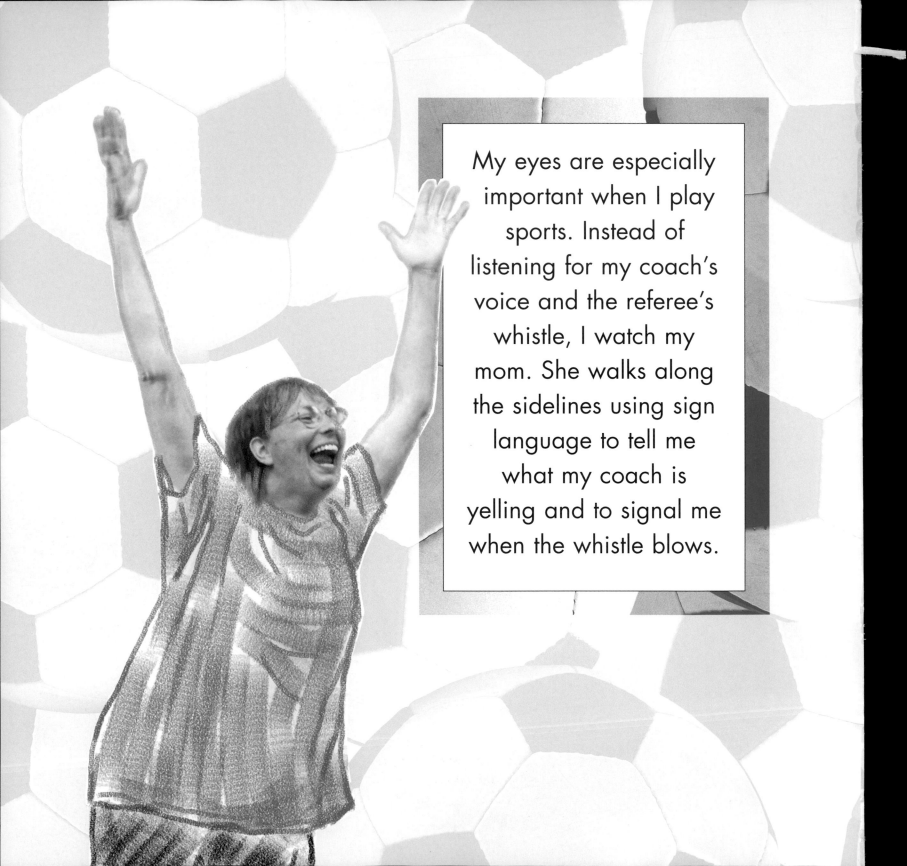

My eyes are especially important when I play sports. Instead of listening for my coach's voice and the referee's whistle, I watch my mom. She walks along the sidelines using sign language to tell me what my coach is yelling and to signal me when the whistle blows.

Most kids I play against never even realize that I am deaf. They usually ask, "Who's the lady on the sideline waving her arms around?"

"That's my mom," I tell them.

Like my brothers and sister, I have to get up early to go to school. My sister wakes up to her clock radio, and my brothers use an alarm clock with a bell. I have a special alarm that I put inside my pillowcase. When it is time for me to wake up, it shakes my pillow.

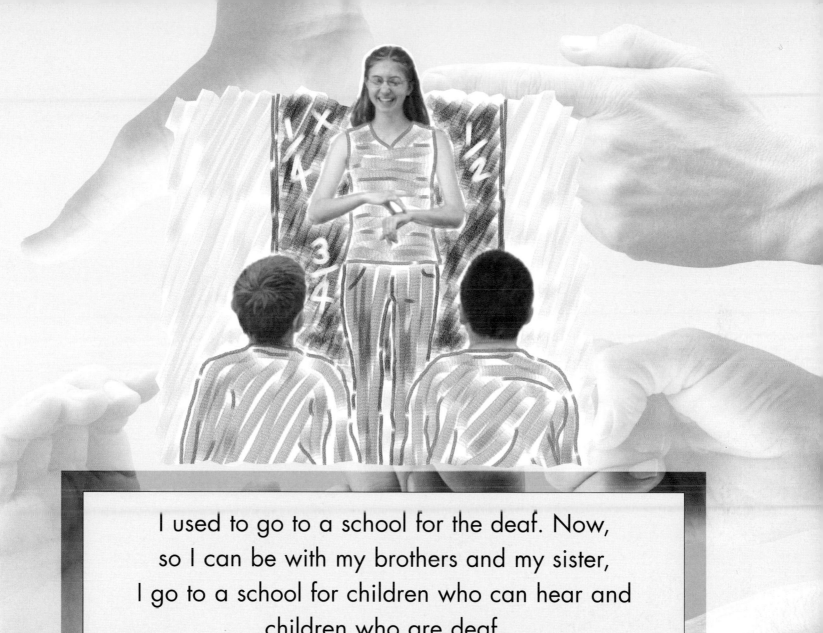

I used to go to a school for the deaf. Now,
so I can be with my brothers and my sister,
I go to a school for children who can hear and
children who are deaf.
I sit in the front row across from Robyn, my interpreter.
She signs what my teacher and the other students
are saying. I never feel left out when Robyn is around.

I have lots of friends at school. Dominic is my best hearing friend. I taught him some words in sign language.

First, I showed him how to sign his name. He caught on quickly and signed his name back to me.

Then I showed him how to sign the words "different" and "same." I taught him "different" because we look different. I taught him "same" because he and I both like the same sport—soccer. But the best word I taught him is "friend."

I have another friend, Samantha, who is deaf like I am. She learned sign language as a baby, too. I got to know Samantha because we both love to act. We have appeared in many plays. Like hearing actors, we memorize our parts. But instead of using our voices to say the words, we sign them with our hands.

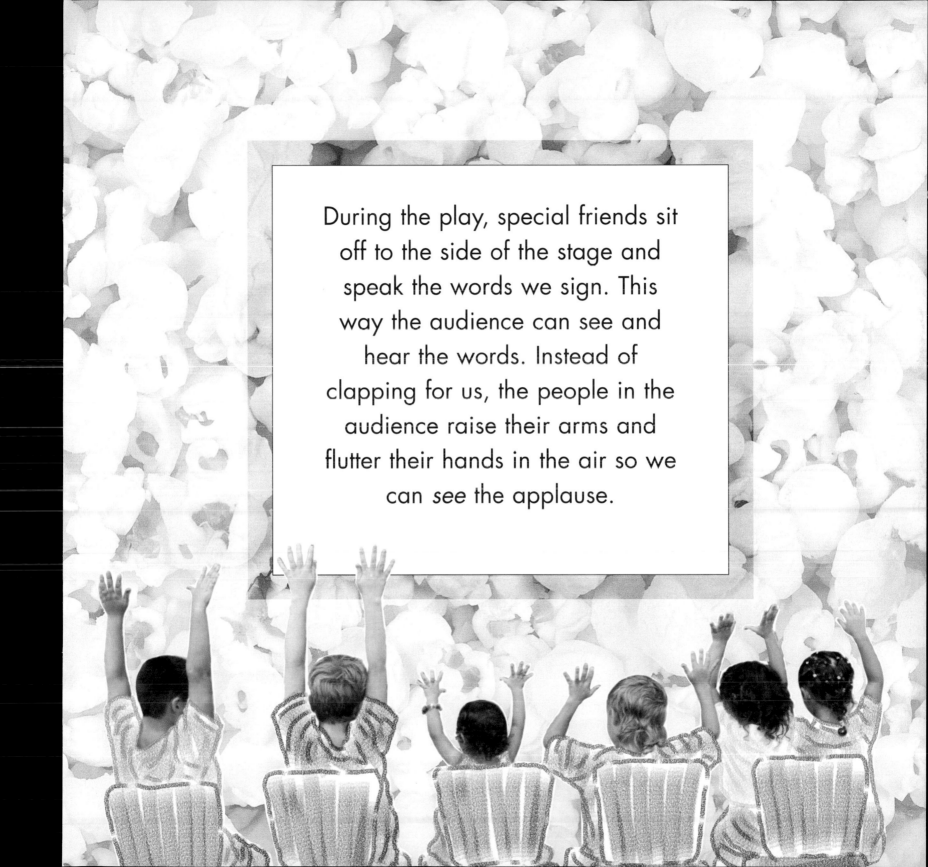

During the play, special friends sit off to the side of the stage and speak the words we sign. This way the audience can see and hear the words. Instead of clapping for us, the people in the audience raise their arms and flutter their hands in the air so we can *see* the applause.

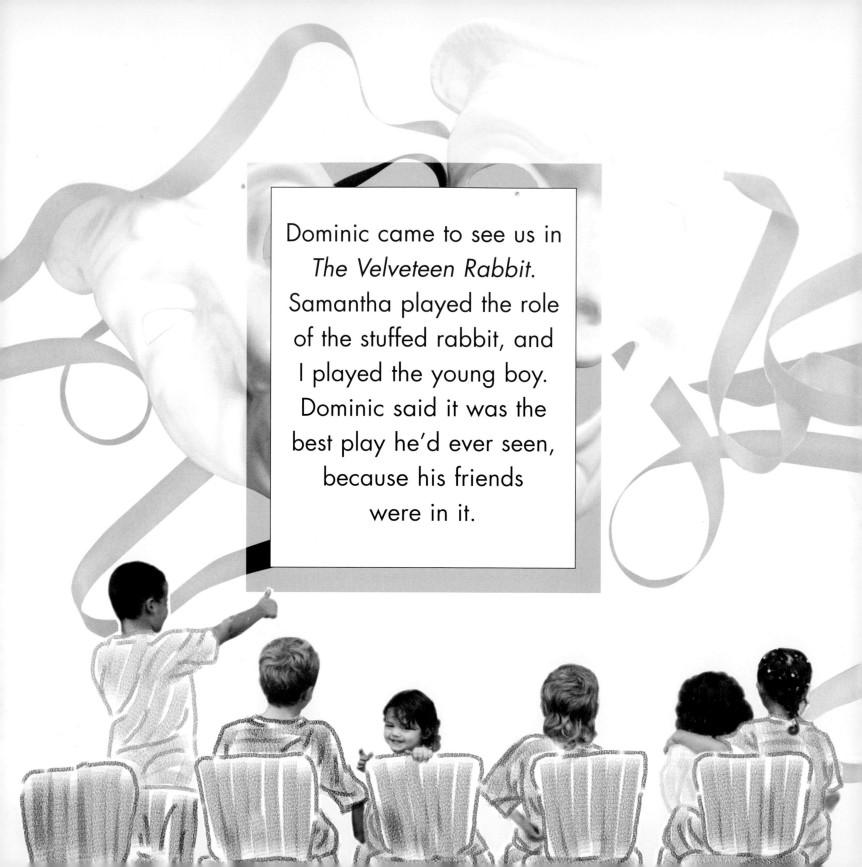

Dominic came to see us in *The Velveteen Rabbit.* Samantha played the role of the stuffed rabbit, and I played the young boy. Dominic said it was the best play he'd ever seen, because his friends were in it.

My doctors, my interpreter, and special devices like
my hearing aids help me in many ways.
I can go to the same school as my brothers and
my sister. I play soccer and act in a children's
theater. I've made many friends, and
we have a lot in common.

We're also different. Dominic and I like soccer, but Samantha prefers roller-blading. Samantha and I like to act, but Dominic would rather draw. Samantha and I are deaf, but Dominic is hearing.

Same. Different.

Sometimes I wonder what it would be like to hear. I once asked Dominic if sunlight makes a noise when it shines through the clouds or hits the sidewalk. He shook his head no.

"Can you hear a rainbow?" I asked him. "Does it make a noise?"
"No," he said, "some things don't need a noise. A rainbow is just the same for you and me."

One thing I know for sure—I do not need
to hear sounds to know I have a friend.
I hook my finger on Dominic's, and
together we sign "friend."